Prayers

THE FRUITFUL HEART

January February March

DEVOTIONS BY CHRISTAL SHARP

Blessed is the man
who does not walk in the counsel of the
wicked, or set foot on the path of sinners, or
sit in the seat of mockers. But his delight is in
the Law of the LORD, and on His law he
meditates day and night. He is like a tree
planted by streams of water, yielding its fruit
in season, whose leaf does not wither, and
who prospers in all he does.
Psalm 1:1-3 BSB

TENDER HEARTS PRESS

January 2nd.

I HAVE TOLD YOU THESE THINGS SO
THAT IN ME YOU MAY HAVE PEACE.
IN THE WORLD YOU WILL HAVE
TRIBULATION. BUT TAKE COURAGE;
I HAVE OVERCOME THE WORLD!"
JOHN 16:33 BSB

Daily Meditation:
Heavenly Father, I praise Your name. You meet me in my troubles, and comfort me. Lord, thank You that Your peace is not dependent on my circumstances, and that in You I will have victory over my life.

Additional Readings:
1 John 4:4 | John 14:27

Bible in a year:
Genesis Chapters: 4 - 7

January 3rd.

"May the LORD bless you and keep you; may the LORD cause His face to shine upon you and be gracious to you; may the LORD lift up His countenance toward you and give you peace."

Numbers 6:24-26 esv

Daily Meditation:
Father God, I am grateful to be Your child, thank You for loving me and for pouring Your grace and mercy into my life. Your blessings and provision show me Your great care for me and my family.

Additional Readings:
Psalm 80:19 | Exodus 33:19

Bible in a year:
Genesis Chapters: 8 - 11

January

In peace I will both lie
down and sleep, for You
alone, O Lord, make me
dwell in safety.
Psalm 4:8 ESV

Peace

January 1st.

I WILL LEAD THE BLIND BY A WAY THEY DID NOT KNOW; I WILL GUIDE THEM ON UNFAMILIAR PATHS. I WILL TURN DARKNESS INTO LIGHT BEFORE THEM AND ROUGH PLACES INTO LEVEL GROUND. THESE THINGS I WILL DO FOR THEM, AND I WILL NOT FORSAKE THEM.

ISAIAH 42:16 BSB

Daily Meditation:

Lord, thank You for loving me, and not leaving me to wander alone. I ask for Your guidance and wisdom to lead me. I ask for Your peace to surround me. I ask for clarity to discern Your will for my life.

Additional Readings:
Isaiah 48:17-19 | Luke 3:4-6

Bible in a year:
Genesis Chapters: 1 - 3

Fruit of the Spirit
Seasonal Devotional

January
Peace
Lavender

February
Love
Rose

March
Temperance
Daisy

"I AM THE TRUE VINE, AND MY FATHER IS THE KEEPER OF THE VINEYARD. HE CUTS OFF EVERY BRANCH IN ME THAT BEARS NO FRUIT, AND EVERY BRANCH THAT DOES BEAR FRUIT, HE PRUNES TO MAKE IT EVEN MORE FRUITFUL. YOU ARE ALREADY CLEAN BECAUSE OF THE WORD I HAVE SPOKEN TO YOU. REMAIN IN ME, AND I WILL REMAIN IN YOU. JUST AS NO BRANCH CAN BEAR FRUIT BY ITSELF UNLESS IT REMAINS IN THE VINE, NEITHER CAN YOU BEAR FRUIT UNLESS YOU REMAIN IN ME."

JOHN 15:1-4

Heavenly Father,
We come before You with hearts open to Your Word and Your Spirit. We seek deeper understanding, wisdom and Your guidance. Your Word tells us that 'the fruit of the Spirit is love, joy, peace, forbearance, kindness, goodness, faithfulness, gentleness and self-control' (Galatians 5:22-23).
Lord, help us to cultivate these gifts within us, so that our lives may bring glory to Your name. Your Word is a lamp to our feet and a light to our path (Psalm 119:105). As we listen and obey, may we grow in our ability to walk in step with the Spirit, letting Your peace rule in our hearts and Your Word dwell richly in our lives (Colossians 3:15-16). Transform us, Lord, so that through our obedience, we may enrich the lives of others and be a living testimony of Your love and grace.
We ask this in the name of Jesus,
Amen.

January 6th.

THE LORD IS MY CHOSEN PORTION AND MY CUP; YOU HAVE MADE MY LOT SECURE. THE LINES OF MY BOUNDARY HAVE FALLEN IN PLEASANT PLACES; SURELY MY INHERITANCE IS DELIGHTFUL. I WILL BLESS THE LORD WHO COUNSELS ME; EVEN AT NIGHT MY CONSCIENCE INSTRUCTS ME.
PSALM 16:5-8 ESV

Daily Meditation:
Father God, You are my provider and I trust in You to meet my needs. Your blessings are many and I am humbled by Your love and concern, not leaving me alone to fend for myself but providing richly in Your grace and mercy.

Additional Readings:
Psalm 23:5 | Jeremiah 3:19

Bible in a year:
Genesis Chapters: 20 - 22

January 7th.

NOW MAY THE GOD OF HOPE FILL YOU
WITH ALL JOY AND PEACE AS YOU
BELIEVE IN HIM, SO THAT YOU MAY
OVERFLOW WITH HOPE BY THE POWER
OF THE HOLY SPIRIT.

ROMANS 15:13 BSB

Daily Meditation:
Holy Spirit, calm my heart and mind, guide me through life's
challenges with serenity. Help me to trust in Your plan and
find solace in Your presence. In Jesus' name, I pray. Amen.

Additional Readings:
Philippians 2:14-18

Bible in a year:
Genesis Chapters: 23 -24

January 4th.

I love You, O LORD, my strength.
The LORD is my rock, my fortress,
and my deliverer. My God is my
rock, in whom I take refuge,
my shield, and the horn of my
salvation, my stronghold.
Psalm 18:1-2 esv

Daily Meditation:
Father God, You are good. You give me strength
when I am weak. Shelter and protect me when I am
vulnerable. You heal my wounds and hide me in the
shadow of Your wings.

Additional Readings:
Psalm 19:14 | Jeremiah 16:19

Bible in a year:
Genesis Chapters: 12 - 15

January 5th.

Now may the God of peace Himself sanctify you completely, and may your entire spirit, soul, and body be kept blameless at the coming of our Lord Jesus Christ. The One who calls you is faithful, and He will do it.
1 Thessalonians 5:23-24 esv

Daily Meditation:
Heavenly Father, You are faithful, and I trust that You will complete the good work You have begun in me. Strengthen me, O Lord, to walk in obedience and holiness, and may Your grace sustain me every step of the way.

Additional Readings:
1 Corinthians 1:8 | Romans 16:20

Bible in a year:
Genesis Chapters: 16 - 19

January 8th.

"COME TO ME, ALL YOU WHO ARE
WEARY AND BURDENED, AND I WILL
GIVE YOU REST."
MATTHEW 11:28 BSB

Daily Meditation:
Lord, I am grateful that when my days are long and my
responsibilities mounting; Father that I can bring my cares to
You. Thank You for providing times of respite and peace in
this life and the next to come.

Additional Readings:
Psalm 121:8 | Colossians 3:23

Bible in a year:
Genesis Chapters: 25 - 26

January 9th.

Yet a little while, and the wicked will be no more; though you look for them, they will not be found. But the meek will inherit the land and delight themselves in abundant peace.

Psalm 37:10-11 ESV

Daily Meditation:
Father God, I long for a world that is truly peaceful, but until then, thank You for being my shield and refuge in this life. I put my hope in a peaceful eternity spent basking in the glory of Your presence.

Additional Readings:
Psalm 37:34-40

Bible in a year:
Genesis Chapters: 27 - 29

January 10th.

Do you not know? Have you not heard? The LORD is the everlasting God, the Creator of the ends of the earth. He will not grow tired or weary; His understanding is beyond searching out. He gives power to the faint and increases the strength of the weak.

Isaiah 40:28-29 BSB

Daily Meditation:
Lord, when life feels hard, please help me to remember to come to You first to receive Your strength and peace. I need Your grace, guidance and provision. Help me to wait on You.

Additional Readings:
Psalm 90:2 | Psalm 147:5

Bible in a year:
Genesis Chapters: 30 - 31

January 11th.

FOR UNTO US A CHILD IS BORN, UNTO US A SON IS GIVEN, AND THE GOVERNMENT WILL BE UPON HIS SHOULDERS. AND HE WILL BE CALLED WONDERFUL COUNSELOR, MIGHTY GOD, EVERLASTING FATHER, PRINCE OF PEACE.

ISAIAH 9:6 BSB

Daily Meditation:

Jesus, thank You for coming into this world to be an example of what love, peace and sacrifice look like. Fill me with Your power so that I may be a light to those around me.

Additional Readings:
Isaiah 9:7 | Matthew 1:20-23

Bible in a year:
Genesis Chapters: 32 -34

January 12th.

FINALLY, BROTHERS, REJOICE. AIM FOR RESTORATION, COMFORT ONE ANOTHER, AGREE WITH ONE ANOTHER, LIVE IN PEACE; AND THE GOD OF LOVE AND PEACE WILL BE WITH YOU.

2 CORINTHIANS 13:11 ESV

Daily Meditation:
Father God, thank You for showing me the way of love.
May I be quick to forgive and be patient with those around me. Thank You for blessing me with Your peace.

Additional Readings:
Roman 14:10 | Romans 15:5-7

Bible in a year:
Genesis Chapters: 35 - 37

January 13th.

THEREFORE WE DO NOT LOSE HEART. THOUGH OUR OUTER SELF IS WASTING AWAY, YET OUR INNER SELF IS BEING RENEWED DAY BY DAY. FOR OUR LIGHT AND MOMENTARY AFFLICTION IS PRODUCING FOR US AN ETERNAL WEIGHT OF GLORY THAT IS FAR BEYOND COMPARISON.
2 CORINTHIANS 4:16-17 BSB

Daily Meditation:
Heavenly Father, teach me to see beyond the temporary, to fix my eyes on the unseen and everlasting. I trust in Your promises and hold fast to the assurance that my present struggles are achieving a greater purpose.

Additional Readings:
Isaiah 40:29 | Isaiah 40:31

Bible in a year:
Genesis Chapters: 38 - 40

January 14th.

But the fruit of the Spirit is love, joy, peace, patience, kindness, goodness, faithfulness, gentleness, and self-control. Against such things there is no law.

Galatians 5:22-23 BSB

Daily Meditation:

Holy Spirit, I ask that You cultivate in me a renewed mind. Doing away with trying to satisfy my flesh, living selfishly or harboring unforgiveness or anger. May I learn to walk in the Spirit so that I may produce good fruit.

Additional Readings:
Psalm 29:11 | Galatians 5:16-21

Bible in a year:
Genesis Chapters: 41 - 42

January 15th.

NOW MAY THE LORD OF PEACE
HIMSELF GIVE YOU PEACE AT ALL
TIMES AND IN EVERY WAY. THE LORD
BE WITH ALL OF YOU.
2 THESSALONIANS 3:16 BSB

Daily Meditation:
In every moment of my life, I seek the peace that only You
can give. When I feel anxious or burdened, remind me that
You are always with me, ready to calm my heart and guide
my steps. Help me to trust in Your timing and provision.

Additional Readings:
John 14:6 | Romans 5:1-2

Bible in a year:
Genesis Chapters: 43 - 45

January 16th.

Though the mountains may be removed and the hills may be shaken, My loving devotion will not depart from you, and My covenant of peace will not be broken," says the LORD, who has compassion on you.

Isaiah 54:10 BSB

Daily Meditation:
Jesus, I praise Your holy name for You're good and You never change. I am so grateful that my failures and mistakes can't keep me from Your love and grace.

Additional Readings:
Matthew 24:35 | Isaiah 51:6

Bible in a year:
Genesis Chapters: 46 - 47

January 17th.

Then Jesus got up and rebuked the wind and the sea. "Silence!" He commanded. "Be still!" And the wind died down, and it was perfectly calm. "Why are you so afraid?" He asked. "Do you still have no faith?"

Mark 4:39-40 BSB

Daily Meditation:
When the storms of life and winds of trouble come and try to steal my peace; let me remember and believe that You Lord are in control. You're faithful to guide and protect me and peace is found in You.

Additional Readings:
Psalm 65:7-8 | 1 Peter 5:7-9

Bible in a year:
Genesis Chapters: 48 - 50

January 18th.

You will keep in perfect peace the steadfast of mind, because he trusts in You. Trust in the LORD forever, because GOD the LORD is the Rock eternal.

Isaiah 26:3-4 BSB

Daily Meditation:
Lord, thank You for being a tower of protection in my life and for giving me strength when I am tired and weak. Thank You for hearing me when I call out to You Father and meeting me in my troubles with Your grace and provision.

Additional Readings:
Psalm 55:22 | Psalm 62:5-8

Bible in a year:
Exodus Chapters: 1 - 3

January 19th.

RECONCILE NOW AND BE AT PEACE WITH HIM; THEREBY GOOD WILL COME TO YOU. RECEIVE INSTRUCTION FROM HIS MOUTH, AND LAY UP HIS WORDS IN YOUR HEART. IF YOU RETURN TO THE ALMIGHTY, YOU WILL BE RESTORED.

JOB 22:21-23 BSB

Daily Meditation:

Father God, I give You my life and ask that my will be attuned to Yours. Lord Your words are like treasures that sustain me. let Your words be ever present on my mind, let my tongue be willing to speak of Your truth and love.

Additional Readings:

John 17:6-8 | Proverbs 2:1-10

Bible in a year:

Exodus Chapters: 4 - 6

January 20th.

Now may the God of peace, who through the blood of the eternal covenant brought back from the dead our Lord Jesus, that great Shepherd of the sheep, equip you with every good thing to do His will...

Hebrews 13:20-21 BSB

Daily Meditation:
Jesus, thank You for Your sacrifice that brought me into everlasting peace. Lord let the works of my hands and the words of my mouth be pleasing to You, Lord that You would be blessed and glorified.

Additional Readings:
Isaiah 55:3 | Galatians 6:7-9

Bible in a year:
Exodus Chapters: 7 - 9

January 21st.

PEACEMAKERS WHO SOW IN PEACE REAP THE FRUIT OF RIGHTEOUSNESS.

JAMES 3:18 BSB

Daily Meditation:

Jesus, thank You for showing me the way of true love and peace. Lord, I want to bear good fruit so that those around me will take notice and see what You have worked in me. Help me to life in peace with all those around me.

Additional Readings:
Hebrews 12:11 | Hosea 10:12

Bible in a year:
Exodus Chapters: 10 - 12

January 22nd.

THE WORK OF RIGHTEOUSNESS WILL
BE PEACE; THE SERVICE OF
RIGHTEOUSNESS WILL BE QUIET
CONFIDENCE FOREVER. THEN MY
PEOPLE WILL DWELL IN A PEACEFUL
PLACE, IN SAFE AND SECURE
PLACES OF REST
ISAIAH 32:17–18 BSB

Daily Meditation:
Lord, thank You that Your righteousness worked in me by
the Holy Spirit, brings me peace now in this life. I put my
hope and trust in You for eternal peace and rest.

Additional Readings:
Isaiah 11:1-9

Bible in a year:
Exodus Chapters: 13 - 15

January 23rd.

I WILL LISTEN TO WHAT GOD THE LORD WILL SAY, FOR HE WILL SURELY SPEAK PEACE TO HIS PEOPLE AND HIS SAINTS; HE WILL NOT LET THEM RETURN TO FOLLY. SURELY HIS SALVATION IS NEAR TO THOSE WHO FEAR HIM, THAT HIS GLORY MAY DWELL IN OUR LAND.

PSALM 85:8-9 BSB

Daily Meditation:
Lord God, I think of all the ways I have walked that were foolish and I think of all the times You have shown Your loving kindness and mercy. Leading me with Your word, gently back to You, where I am safe and secure.

Additional Readings:
2 Peter 2:21 | Ezekiel 14:6-7

Bible in a year:
Exodus Chapters: 16 - 18

January 24th.

THEREFORE, AS GOD'S CHOSEN PEOPLE, HOLY AND DEARLY LOVED, CLOTHE YOURSELVES WITH COMPASSION, KINDNESS, HUMILITY, GENTLENESS AND PATIENCE. BEAR WITH EACH OTHER AND FORGIVE ONE ANOTHER IF ANY OF YOU HAS A GRIEVANCE AGAINST SOMEONE. FORGIVE AS THE LORD FORGAVE YOU.
COLOSSIANS 3:12-13 BSB

Daily Meditation:
Lord, I want to radiate Your love and be a light in this world, that at times seems so dark. Help me to walk in the way of peace and remember to extend grace and mercy to others.

Additional Readings:
1 Corinthians 13:2-7

Bible in a year:
Exodus Chapters: 19 - 21

January 25th.

"BECAUSE OF THE TENDER MERCY OF OUR GOD, BY WHICH THE RISING SUN WILL COME TO US FROM HEAVEN TO SHINE ON THOSE LIVING IN DARKNESS AND IN THE SHADOW OF DEATH, TO GUIDE OUR FEET INTO THE PATH OF PEACE."

LUKE 1:78-79 BSB

Daily Meditation:

Father, in Your merciful love You sent Your son to be the one to lead us back to You. Jesus, You are the way, the truth and the life. You are my healer, provider and lover of my soul. Thank You for bringing me into the presence of the Father.

Additional Readings:
Psalm 25:6 | Ephesians 5:14

Bible in a year:
Exodus Chapters: 22 - 24

January 26th.

I URGE YOU, FIRST OF ALL, TO PRAY FOR ALL PEOPLE. ASK GOD TO HELP THEM; INTERCEDE ON THEIR BEHALF AND GIVE THANKS FOR THEM. PRAY THIS WAY FOR KINGS AND ALL WHO ARE IN AUTHORITY SO THAT WE CAN LIVE PEACEFUL AND QUIET LIVES MARKED BY GODLINESS AND DIGNITY.
1 TIMOTHY 2:1-2 NLT

Daily Meditation:
Lord Jesus, I pray that You would bring to mind those I should pray for whether family, friend, stranger, King or country; that You would lay them on my heart and that I would be obedient to pray for them.

Additional Readings:
Jeremiah 29:7 | Psalm 122:6-9

Bible in a year:
Exodus Chapters: 25 - 27

January 27th.

Exalt the LORD, O Jerusalem.
praise Your God, O Zion! For He
strengthens the bars of your
gates and blesses the children
within You. He makes peace at
your borders; He fills you with
the finest wheat.
Psalm 147:12-14 BSB

Daily Meditation:
Lord God, You are so good! I praise You for Your faithfulness,
provision and protection. I come to You humbly and ask for
Your grace and mercy to wash me clean. Fill my spirit anew
strengthen me and guide me all the days of my life.

Additional Readings:
Psalm 51:1-19

Bible in a year:
Exodus Chapters: 28 - 29

January 28th.

HE WILL BLESS THOSE WHO FEAR THE
LORD, SMALL AND GREAT ALIKE.
MAY THE LORD GIVE YOU INCREASE,
BOTH YOU AND YOUR CHILDREN.
MAY YOU BE BLESSED BY THE LORD,
THE MAKER OF HEAVEN AND EARTH.

PSALM 115:13-15 BSB

Daily Meditation:
Your Blessings over my life Lord are many. Your provision is
what I need and more, Your presence fills me with peace.
Your goodness and love follow me all my days. Praise be to
the God most high!

Additional Readings:
Isaiah 57:14-16 | Nehemiah 9:6

Bible in a year:
Exodus Chapters: 30 - 32

January 29th.

Never pay back evil with more evil. Do things in such a way that everyone can see you are honorable. Do all that you can to live in peace with everyone.
Romans 12:17-18 NLT

Daily Meditation:
Holy Spirit, help me to forgive and heal from the past wounds inflicted by those who have hurt or wronged me. In Your grace and love Lord, fill me with Your peace to be able to love those all around me, even my enemie.

Additional Readings:
Proverbs 20:22 | 1 Peter 3:8-10

Bible in a year:
Exodus Chapters: 33 - 35

January 30th.

SO IF YOU ARE OFFERING YOUR GIFT AT THE ALTAR AND THERE REMEMBER THAT YOUR BROTHER HAS SOMETHING AGAINST YOU, LEAVE YOUR GIFT THERE BEFORE THE ALTAR. FIRST GO AND BE RECONCILED TO YOUR BROTHER; THEN COME AND OFFER YOUR GIFT.
MATTHEW 5:23-24 BSB

Daily Meditation:
Lord, Your mercy is so worthy of all our praise, You are so faithful to forgive. Thank You for teaching me to walk humbly, to forgive and love others. Let my life be a praise offering to You.

Additional Readings:
Mark 11:25 | Matthew 6:14

Bible in a year:
Exodus Chapters: 36 - 38

January 31st.

BLESSED ARE THE MERCIFUL, FOR
THEY WILL BE SHOWN MERCY.
BLESSED ARE THE PURE IN HEART, FOR
THEY WILL SEE GOD. BLESSED ARE
THE PEACEMAKERS, FOR THEY WILL BE
CALLED SONS OF GOD....
MATTHEW 5:7-9 BSB

Daily Meditation:
All the days of my life Lord, let me bear good fruit for You. Let
my life be a blessing to others an offering of love, joy, peace,
patience, kindness, goodness, faithfulness, gentleness and
self-control.

Additional Readings:
Psalm 24:4 | Romans 8:14

Bible in a year:
Exodus Chapters: 39 - 40

February

"You must love the Lord your God with all your heart, all your soul, and all Your mind. This is the first and greatest commandment. A second is equally important Love your neighbor as yourself..."
Matthew 22:37-40 NLT

Love

February 1st.

BUT YOU, MAN OF GOD, FLEE FROM ALL THIS, AND PURSUE RIGHTEOUSNESS, GODLINESS, FAITH, LOVE, ENDURANCE, AND GENTLENESS.

1 TIMOTHY 6:11 NIV

Daily Meditation:
Lord Jesus, may Your Holy Spirit guide my thoughts and actions. May I grow spiritually and emotionally to be more like You in all aspects of my life. Help me to radiate Your love for the world.

Additional Readings:
1 Timothy 6:9-10

Bible in a year:
Leviticus Chapters: 1 - 4

February 2nd.

"AND WE HAVE COME TO KNOW AND BELIEVE THE LOVE THAT GOD HAS FOR US. GOD IS LOVE; WHOEVER ABIDES IN LOVE ABIDES IN GOD, AND GOD IN HIM."

1 JOHN 4:16 BSB

Daily Meditation:
My Lord, thank You for teaching me what love is so that I can be more loving to those around me. Let my heart be open to generously share that love with others.

Additional Readings:
1 John 4:7-13

Bible in a year:
Leviticus Chapters: 5 - 7

February 3rd.

As the Father has loved Me, so have I loved you. Remain in My love. If you keep My commandments, you will remain in My love, just as I have kept My Father's commandments and remain in His love.

John 15:9-10 BSB

Daily Meditation:
Lord Jesus, empower me to love others with the selfless and sacrificial love that mirrors Your own. Help me to walk with You and grow in Your spiritual guidance so I may discern how to effectively love others.

Additional Readings:
John 15:5-8

Bible in a year:
Leviticus Chapters: 8 - 10

February 4th.

... AND ANY OTHER COMMANDMENTS,
ARE SUMMED UP IN THIS ONE DECREE:
"LOVE YOUR NEIGHBOR AS YOURSELF."
LOVE DOES NO WRONG TO ITS
NEIGHBOR. THEREFORE LOVE IS THE
FULFILLMENT OF THE LAW.
ROMANS 13:9-10 BSB

Daily Meditation:
Lord Jesus, May my heart overflow with unconditional love,
understanding that pure love transcends differences in
beliefs and embraces all with light and kindness. May my
capacity for compassion and love grow more each day.

Additional Readings:
Leviticus 19:18 | Mark 12:31

Bible in a year:
Leviticus Chapters: 11 - 13

February 5th.

BE IMITATORS OF GOD, THEREFORE, AS BELOVED CHILDREN, AND WALK IN LOVE, JUST AS CHRIST LOVED US AND GAVE HIMSELF UP FOR US AS A FRAGRANT SACRIFICIAL OFFERING TO GOD.

EPHESIANS 5:1-2 BSB

Daily Meditation:

Gracious God, may we walk in the way of love, following Your example of selfless giving for the benefit of others. May I be a beacon of Your love in this world.

Additional Readings:
1 Peter 1:22-23

Bible in a year:
Leviticus Chapters: 14 - 15

February 6th.

IF I SPEAK IN THE TONGUES OF MEN
AND OF ANGELS, BUT HAVE NOT LOVE,
I AM ONLY A RINGING GONG OR A
CLANGING CYMBAL.

1 CORINTHIANS 13:1 BSB

Daily Meditation:
Father God, let the words of my mouth and the meditations
of my heart be pleasing to You. May the words I speak
encourage, bring life and be an outpouring of genuine love
towards others that points back to You.

Additional Readings:
1 John 4:20-21

Bible in a year:
Leviticus Chapters: 16 - 18

February 7th.

IF I HAVE THE GIFT OF PROPHECY
AND CAN FATHOM ALL MYSTERIES AND
ALL KNOWLEDGE, AND IF I HAVE
ABSOLUTE FAITH SO AS TO MOVE
MOUNTAINS, BUT HAVE NOT LOVE, I
AM NOTHING.
1 CORINTHIANS 13:2 BSB

Daily Meditation:
Father God, I pray for not only discernment in understanding
the whispers of Your word but also a heart to do what You
say. Please help me to lead those around me by example
through love and faith.

Additional Readings:
1 Peter 4:11 | 1 Corinthians 12:8-10

Bible in a year:
Leviticus Chapters: 19 - 21

February 8th.

IF I GIVE ALL I POSSESS TO THE POOR
AND EXULT IN THE SURRENDER OF MY
BODY, BUT HAVE NOT LOVE, I GAIN
NOTHING.

1 CORINTHIANS 13:3 BSB

Daily Meditation:
Lord Jesus, let me not boast of my good deeds and in no one
but You. In trials and suffering I ask that You would
strengthen me with Your Spirit to love even those who are
difficult and hard to love.

Additional Readings:
1 Peter 1:3-12

Bible in a year:
Leviticus Chapters: 22 - 23

February 9th.

LOVE IS PATIENT, LOVE IS KIND. IT DOES NOT ENVY, IT DOES NOT BOAST, IT IS NOT PROUD. IT IS NOT RUDE, IT IS NOT SELF-SEEKING, IT IS NOT EASILY ANGERED, IT KEEPS NO ACCOUNT OF WRONGS. LOVE TAKES NO PLEASURE IN EVIL, BUT REJOICES IN THE TRUTH. IT BEARS ALL THINGS, BELIEVES ALL THINGS, HOPES ALL THINGS, ENDURES ALL THINGS.
1 CORINTHIANS 13:4-7 BSB

Daily Meditation:
Lord, thank You for teaching me what love really is. I ask You to empower me when I struggle to love others as You have loved me. Let my love cause ripples of positive change for those affected by me.

Additional Readings:
1 Peter 4:8-10

Bible in a year:
Leviticus Chapters: 24 - 25

February 10th.

AND WE KNOW THAT GOD WORKS ALL
THINGS TOGETHER FOR THE GOOD OF
THOSE WHO LOVE HIM, WHO ARE
CALLED ACCORDING TO HIS PURPOSE.
ROMANS 8:28 BSB

Daily Meditation:
Father God, thank You for the reassurance that You can turn
even the bad things around to bring about good. Although
hard times will come, I praise You for Your loving kindness
towards us in how You work all things out.

Additional Readings:
Romans 8:31-35

Bible in a year:
Leviticus Chapters: 26 - 27

February 11th.

If you love those who love you, what credit is that to you? Even sinners love those who love them. And if you do good to those who are good to you, what credit is that to You? Even sinners do the same.

Luke 6:32-33 BSB

Daily Meditation:
Lord, living in this world, it is so easy to be self centered. Guide and teach me to love and give even when I have nothing to gain. Let my life be an offering to do Your will.

Additional Readings:
Luke 6:27-31

Bible in a year:
Numbers Chapters: 1 - 2

February 12th.

THERE IS NO FEAR IN LOVE, BUT PERFECT LOVE DRIVES OUT FEAR, BECAUSE FEAR INVOLVES PUNISHMENT. THE ONE WHO FEARS HAS NOT BEEN PERFECTED IN LOVE. WE LOVE BECAUSE HE FIRST LOVED US.

1 JOHN 4:18-19 BSB

Daily Meditation:
Heavenly Father, Thank You for Your unfailing love, help me to live without fear and anxiety, knowing that You are with me. May I be filled with Your love, so that fear has no place in my heart.

Additional Readings:

1 John 4:10

Bible in a year:
Numbers Chapters: 3 - 4

February 13th.

Do not love the world or anything in the world. If anyone loves the world, the love of the Father is not in him. For all that is in the world, the desires of the flesh, the desires of the eyes, and the pride of life, is not from the Father but from the world.

1 John 2:15-16 BSB

Daily Meditation:
Holy Spirit, I ask for You to strengthen me when temptation comes. For the desires or the heart are many and easily pull me from Your will for my life. Let me seek the eternal over the temporal, Your will over my own.

Additional Readings:
Romans 12:2 | John 15:18-21

Bible in a year:
Numbers Chapters: 5-6

February 14th.

By this we know what love is: Jesus laid down His life for us, and we ought to lay down our lives for our brothers. If anyone with earthly possessions sees his brother in need, but withholds his compassion from him, how can the love of God abide in him?

1 John 3:16-17 BSB

Daily Meditation:
Lord, help me to be selfless in a world that rewards selfishness. Let me be attuned to Your will, so that I can be Your hands and feet and meet the needs of others.

Additional Readings:
1 John 3:18-19 | John 10:11

Bible in a year:
Numbers Chapters: 7

February 15th.

But if anyone keeps His word, the love of God has been truly perfected in him. By this we know that we are in Him. Whoever claims to abide in Him must walk as Jesus walked.

1 John 2:5-6 bsb

Daily Meditation:
Lord Jesus, let me not just hear Your words. Lord let them sink down and saturate my being, so that I am compelled to do Your will, to move as You move, inspired to act by the Holy Spirit.

Additional Readings:
1 John 2:1-4

Bible in a year:
Numbers Chapters: 8-10

February 16th.

Let us not grow weary in well-doing, for in due time we will reap a harvest if we do not give up. Therefore, as we have opportunity, let us do good to everyone, and especially to the family of faith.
Galatians 6:9-10 BSB

Daily Meditation:
Lord, I want to be a light in this world; to help, heal and share Your love. Help me to rely and wait on Your prompting and strength, so I don't grow weary in doing the good works You have set before me.

Additional Readings:
Matthew 10:5-8 | Matthew 10:40-41

Bible in a year:
Numbers Chapters: 11 - 13

February 17th.

IN THE SAME WAY, LET YOUR LIGHT
SHINE BEFORE MEN, THAT THEY MAY
SEE YOUR GOOD DEEDS AND GLORIFY
YOUR FATHER IN HEAVEN.
MATTHEW 5:16 BSB

Daily Meditation:
Jesus, You are the light of the world. I want to grow in my
relationship and knowledge of You, so I may reflect Your
light and goodness to others sitting in chains and darkness.

Additional Readings:
John 1:1-13 | John 3:18-21

Bible in a year:
Numbers Chapters: 14 - 15

February 18th.

FOR GOD SO LOVED THE WORLD THAT HE GAVE HIS ONE AND ONLY SON, THAT EVERYONE WHO BELIEVES IN HIM SHALL NOT PERISH BUT HAVE ETERNAL LIFE. FOR GOD DID NOT SEND HIS SON INTO THE WORLD TO CONDEMN THE WORLD, BUT TO SAVE THE WORLD THROUGH HIM.

JOHN 3:16-17 BSB

Daily Meditation:
Lord, You are so good! Thank You for paying the price for my sins. None are too great that Your love and sacrifice can't erase them. Thank You for holding me with Your everlasting love and bringing my soul into peace.

Additional Readings:
1 John 4:14 - 15 | Luke 19:10

Bible in a year:
Numbers Chapters: 16 - 17

February 19th.

TRUST IN THE LORD AND DO GOOD;
DWELL IN THE LAND AND CULTIVATE
FAITHFULNESS. DELIGHT YOURSELF IN
THE LORD, AND HE WILL GIVE YOU
THE DESIRES OF YOUR HEART. COMMIT
YOUR WAY TO THE LORD; TRUST IN
HIM, AND HE WILL DO IT.

PSALM 37:3-5 BSB

Daily Meditation:
Lord Jesus, I give You my life, my heart, my finances, my
children, my career; Lord I commit my will and way to You
and Your timing. It is in better hands for You know the
beginning from the end.

Additional Readings:
Psalm 62:8 | Psalm 115:9

Bible in a year:
Numbers Chapters: 18 - 20

February 20th.

AND LET US CONSIDER HOW TO SPUR ONE ANOTHER ON TO LOVE AND GOOD DEEDS. LET US NOT NEGLECT MEETING TOGETHER, AS SOME HAVE MADE A HABIT, BUT LET US ENCOURAGE ONE ANOTHER, AND ALL THE MORE AS YOU SEE THE DAY APPROACHING.
HEBREWS 10:24-25 BSB

Daily Meditation:
Jesus, Thank You for the community of believers You have placed in my life. Let fellowship be a source of strength and encouragement, drawing me closer to You and using my gifts to bless others.

Additional Readings:
Romans 13:11-13 | Hebrew 3:12-14

Bible in a year:
Numbers Chapters: 21 - 22

February 21st.

CONTINUE IN BROTHERLY LOVE. DO NOT NEGLECT TO SHOW HOSPITALITY TO STRANGERS, FOR BY SO DOING SOME PEOPLE HAVE ENTERTAINED ANGELS WITHOUT KNOWING IT.
HEBREWS 13:1-2 BSB

Daily Meditation:
Lord, I pray that in seasons that are dry or abundant that I would be faithful to serve You by helping others. Not just my friends and those I love, but the stranger and wanderer as well.

Additional Readings:
Matthew 25:35 | Titus 1:8

Bible in a year:
Numbers Chapters: 23 - 25

February 22nd.

PRESERVE ME, O GOD, FOR IN YOU I TAKE REFUGE. I SAID TO THE LORD, "YOU ARE MY LORD; APART FROM YOU I HAVE NO GOOD THING." AS FOR THE SAINTS IN THE LAND, THEY ARE THE EXCELLENCE IN WHOM ALL MY DELIGHT RESIDES.

PSALM 16:1-3 BSB

Daily Meditation:

Lord, I praise Your name for all the times You have sheltered me and kept me safe through lifes storms. Even in the struggle there were blessings to light up the dark times. Help me to trust in You always.

Additional Readings:

Psalm 31:1-5

Bible in a year:

Numbers Chapters: 26 - 27

February 23rd.

SING TO HIM A NEW SONG;
PLAY SKILLFULLY WITH A SHOUT OF
JOY. FOR THE WORD OF THE LORD IS
UPRIGHT, AND ALL HIS WORK IS
TRUSTWORTHY. THE LORD LOVES
RIGHTEOUSNESS AND JUSTICE;
THE EARTH IS FULL OF HIS LOVING
DEVOTION.

PSALM 33:3-5 BSB

Daily Meditation:
Gracious Creator, I will lift my voice in praise to You, singing
melodies of joy and gratefulness. Your word is true and
trustworthy, Your deeds are just and faithful. Your love fills
the earth, and Your goodness knows no bounds.

Additional Readings:
Psalm 40:3 | Daniel 4:37

Bible in a year:
Numbers Chapters: 28 - 30

February 24th

Know therefore that the LORD your God is God, the faithful God who keeps His covenant of loving devotion for a thousand generations of those who love Him and keep His commandments.

Deuteronomy 7:9 bsb

Daily Meditation:
Thank You Lord for being patient and guiding me all the days of my life. I am sorry for when I rebelled against You but grateful that You waited, watched over and protected me until I returned to You.

Additional Readings:
Exodus 20:5-6 | Nehemiah 1:5

Bible in a year:
Numbers Chapters: 31 - 32

February 25th.

...THEN YOU, BEING ROOTED AND GROUNDED IN LOVE, WILL HAVE POWER, TOGETHER WITH ALL THE SAINTS, TO COMPREHEND THE LENGTH AND WIDTH AND HEIGHT AND DEPTH OF THE LOVE OF CHRIST...

EPHESIANS 3:17-19 BSB

Daily Meditation:
Father God, when I ponder the depth of Your love; I am humbled by Your devotion to people who constantly go astray. Thank You for making a way to deal with my sin and giving me hope of eternal life with You.

Additional Readings:
Proverbs 8:22-31

Bible in a year:
Numbers Chapters: 33 - 34

February 26th.

... AND TO KNOW THIS LOVE THAT
SURPASSES KNOWLEDGE, THAT YOU
MAY BE FILLED WITH ALL THE
FULLNESS OF GOD. NOW TO HIM WHO
IS ABLE TO DO IMMEASURABLY MORE
THAN ALL WE ASK OR IMAGINE,
ACCORDING TO HIS POWER THAT IS AT
WORK WITHIN US,
EPHESIANS 3:19-20 BSB

Daily Meditation:
Father God, I can look back over the years and think of my
prayers, prayed through tears, frustration and fear. I can see
how You have answered so many of them and more. Your
blessings have been abundant and I am so grateful.

Additional Readings:
Matthew 6:33 | 2 Corinthians 9:8

Bible in a year:
Numbers Chapters: 35 - 36

February 27th.

...."May the beloved of the LORD rest secure in Him; God shields him all day long, and upon His shoulders he rests."

Deuteronomy 33:12 BSB

Daily Meditation:
Jesus, let me always remember the times You turned bad circumstances around into blessings. Let my faith grow that I may boast in You and the love You have towards those who trust and rest in You.

Additional Readings:
Deuteronomy 12:10 | Psalm 91:4

Bible in a year:
Deuteronomy Chapters: 1 - 2

February 28th.

WHO SHALL SEPARATE US FROM THE LOVE OF CHRIST? SHALL TROUBLE OR DISTRESS OR PERSECUTION OR FAMINE OR NAKEDNESS OR DANGER OR SWORD?

ROMANS 8:35 BSB

Daily Meditation:
Thank You Jesus, that even in my trials, failures, sickness, weakness and sin; Lord, You never leave me alone. That is when I actually feel the closest to You, in my need and despair You are always there.

Additional Readings:
Isaiah 43:1-2 | 2 Corinthians 4:7-10

Bible in a year:
Deuteronomy Chapters: 3 - 4

February 29th.

FOR I AM CONVINCED THAT NEITHER
DEATH NOR LIFE, NEITHER ANGELS NOR
PRINCIPALITIES, NEITHER THE PRESENT
NOR THE FUTURE, NOR ANY POWERS,
NEITHER HEIGHT NOR DEPTH, NOR
ANYTHING ELSE IN ALL CREATION, WILL
BE ABLE TO SEPARATE US FROM THE
LOVE OF GOD THAT IS IN CHRIST JESUS
OUR LORD.
ROMANS 8:38-39 BSB

Daily Meditation:
Father God, Your love and kindness towards me is the only
consistent care I have known. Thank You for always being
there for me, holding me up when life gets hard. Speaking
life, strength, healing and provision over me.

Additional Readings:
Romans 5:8 | John 10:27-29

Bible in a year:
Deuteronomy Chapter: 5

March

So you must count yourselves dead to sin but alive to God in Christ Jesus. Therefore do not let sin reign in your mortal body so that you obey its desires.

Romans 6:11-12 BSB

Temperance

March 1st.

DO NOT OFFER ANY PART OF YOURSELF TO SIN AS AN INSTRUMENT OF WICKEDNESS, BUT RATHER OFFER YOURSELVES TO GOD AS THOSE WHO HAVE BEEN BROUGHT FROM DEATH TO LIFE; AND OFFER EVERY PART OF YOURSELF TO HIM AS AN INSTRUMENT OF RIGHTEOUSNESS.

ROMANS 6:13 NIV

Daily Meditation:
Lord, I lay down my life and will and pray that You would use me as an instrument of Your righteousness. I declare that sin has no power over me. I pray that Your grace and unfailing love would flow out of me.

Additional Readings:
Romans 7:5 | Romans 12:1

Bible in a year:
Deuteronomy Chapters: 6-7

March 2nd.

FOR SIN SHALL NO LONGER BE YOUR MASTER, BECAUSE YOU ARE NOT UNDER THE LAW, BUT UNDER GRACE. WHAT THEN? SHALL WE SIN BECAUSE WE ARE NOT UNDER THE LAW BUT UNDER GRACE? BY NO MEANS!

ROMANS 6:14-15 NIV

Daily Meditation:
Lord Jesus help me to walk in the freedom You have given me. May my heart be steadfast, choosing righteousness over bondage of sin. Help me to embrace the abundant life You have offered through grace.

Additional Readings:
Galatians 3:22-23 | Romans 5:17

Bible in a year:
Deuteronomy Chapters: 8-10

March 3rd.

BUT THANKS BE TO GOD THAT, THOUGH YOU USED TO BE SLAVES TO SIN, YOU HAVE COME TO OBEY FROM YOUR HEART THE PATTERN OF TEACHING THAT HAS NOW CLAIMED YOUR ALLEGIANCE. YOU HAVE BEEN SET FREE FROM SIN AND HAVE BECOME SLAVES TO RIGHTEOUSNESS.

ROMANS 6:17-18 NIV

Daily Meditation:
Loving God, thank You for the gift of salvation and the truth that has set me free. Guide me to be obedient from the heart, as I joyfully serve You. Let me not focus on sin which so easily entangles but to keep my eyes on You.

Additional Readings:
2 Corinthians 2:14-17

Bible in a year:
Deuteronomy Chapters: 11-13

March 4th.

BUT NOW THAT YOU HAVE BEEN SET FREE FROM SIN AND HAVE BECOME SLAVES OF GOD, THE BENEFIT YOU REAP LEADS TO HOLINESS, AND THE RESULT IS ETERNAL LIFE. FOR THE WAGES OF SIN IS DEATH, BUT THE GIFT OF GOD IS ETERNAL LIFE IN CHRIST JESUS OUR LORD.
ROMANS 6:22-23 NIV

Daily Meditation:
Gracious Lord, I offer my heartfelt gratitude for the precious gift of eternal life through Jesus Christ my Savior. May I never stray from the path You have chosen for me, so that I may bear the fruit of Your righteousness.

Additional Readings:
John 8:32 | 1 Corinthians 7:22

Bible in a year:
Deuteronomy Chapters: 14-16

March 5th.

But now you must also rid yourselves of all such things as these: anger, rage, malice, slander, and filthy language from your lips. Do not lie to each other, since you have taken off your old self with its practices and have put on the new self, which is being renewed in knowledge in the image of its Creator.

Colossians 3:8-10 NIV

Daily Meditation:
Lord God, I humbly ask for Your strength to rid my heart of anything that is not pleasing to You. Renew my spirit, creating in me a heart of compassion, kindness, and love, so I may reflect Your grace in all my actions and relationships.

Additional Readings:
Psalm 37:7-9

Bible in a year:
Deuteronomy Chapters: 17-20

March 6th.

"... I AM SENDING YOU TO THEM TO OPEN THEIR EYES AND TURN THEM FROM DARKNESS TO LIGHT, AND FROM THE POWER OF SATAN TO GOD, SO THAT THEY MAY RECEIVE FORGIVENESS OF SINS AND A PLACE AMONG THOSE WHO ARE SANCTIFIED BY FAITH IN ME."

ACTS 26:17-18 NIV

Daily Meditation:
Dear Lord, open my eyes to the light of Your truth, turning away from all darkness towards the power of Your grace. Let my will be attuned to Yours, that I may serve You always; so I may have inheritance among those sanctified by faith.

Additional Readings:
Isaiah 29:13-16 | Isaiah 42:7

Bible in a year:
Deuteronomy Chapters: 21-23

March 7th.

...BE CAREFUL THAT YOU DON'T FALL!
NO TEMPTATION HAS OVERTAKEN YOU
EXCEPT WHAT IS COMMON TO MANKIND.
AND GOD IS FAITHFUL; HE WILL NOT LET
YOU BE TEMPTED BEYOND WHAT YOU
CAN BEAR. BUT WHEN YOU ARE
TEMPTED, HE WILL ALSO PROVIDE A
WAY OUT SO THAT YOU CAN ENDURE IT.
1 CORINTHIANS 10:12-13 NIV

Daily Meditation:
Lord, let me be vigilant, never assuming that I am beyond
the reach of temptation. When I face trials, help me to rely
on Your strength, and to practice the gifts of the Spirit. As I
grow in these gifts, may I be closer to You.

Additional Readings:
2 Peter 3:17-18 | Matthew 6:12-13

Bible in a year:
Deuteronomy Chapters: 24-27

March 8th.

"I HAVE THE RIGHT TO DO ANYTHING," YOU SAY BUT NOT EVERYTHING IS BENEFICIAL. "I HAVE THE RIGHT TO DO ANYTHING" BUT NOT EVERYTHING IS CONSTRUCTIVE. NO ONE SHOULD SEEK THEIR OWN GOOD, BUT THE GOOD OF OTHERS.

1 CORINTHIANS 10:23-24 NIV

Daily Meditation:
Father God, help me to seek what is constructive and uplifting. Guide me to prioritize the well-being of those around me, making choices that build up my community. Let my actions always bring glory to You.

Additional Readings:
1 Corinthians 9:22 | Romans 15:1-3

Bible in a year:
Deuteronomy Chapters: 28-29

March 9th.

THEREFORE, I URGE YOU, BROTHERS AND SISTERS, IN VIEW OF GOD'S MERCY, TO OFFER YOUR BODIES AS A LIVING SACRIFICE, HOLY AND PLEASING TO GOD, THIS IS YOUR TRUE AND PROPER WORSHIP.

ROMANS 12:1 NIV

Daily Meditation:
Heavenly Father, I present myself as a living sacrifice, wholly devoted to You. Mold me, guide me, and use my life for Your purpose, that every thought and action may glorify Your name. I seek fellowship with You, speak Lord I am listening.

Additional Readings:
Deuteronomy 14:2 | 2 Cor. 5:1-5

Bible in a year:
Deuteronomy Chapters: 30-31

March 10th.

"ENTER THROUGH THE NARROW GATE.
FOR WIDE IS THE GATE AND BROAD IS
THE ROAD THAT LEADS TO
DESTRUCTION, AND MANY ENTER
THROUGH IT. BUT SMALL IS THE GATE
AND NARROW THE ROAD THAT LEADS
TO LIFE, AND ONLY A FEW FIND IT."
MATTHEW 7:13-14 NIV

Daily Meditation:
Lord, grant me the wisdom and discernment to choose the
narrow path that leads to life. Help me resist the distractions
and temptations that may lead me astray. Guide my steps
towards the enduring joy found in You.

Additional Readings:
Isaiah 35:8 | Luke 13:24

Bible in a year:
Deuteronomy Chapters: 32-34

March 11th.

"By their fruit you will recognize them. Do people pick grapes from thorn bushes, or figs from thistles? Likewise, every good tree bears good fruit, but a bad tree bears bad fruit. A good tree cannot bear bad fruit, and a bad tree cannot bear good fruit."

Matthew 7:16-18 NIV

Daily Meditation:

Lord Jesus, I want those who know me and those who just met me to benefit from the harvest of fruits from my life. Let Your goodness, peace, and genuine love be ever present in me and ready for the picking.

Additional Readings:
Proverbs 20:11 | Matthew 12:33

Bible in a year:
Joshua Chapters: 1-4

March 12th.

"EVERYONE WHO HEARS THESE WORDS OF MINE AND PUTS THEM INTO PRACTICE IS LIKE A WISE MAN WHO BUILT HIS HOUSE ON THE ROCK. THE RAIN CAME DOWN, THE STREAMS ROSE, AND THE WINDS BLEW AND BEAT AGAINST THAT HOUSE; YET IT DID NOT FALL, BECAUSE IT HAD ITS FOUNDATION ON THE ROCK."

MATTHEW 7:24-25 NIV

Daily Meditation:

Jesus, I don't want to be foolish and build my life with my own way and wisdom, I have seen how that goes. Lord I want to build my life on You and every word that comes from Your mouth. That my life will be strong in You.

Additional Readings:
Proverbs 10:8 | Proverbs 12:7

Bible in a year:
Joshua Chapters: 5-8

March 13th.

For the grace of God has appeared that offers salvation to all people. It teaches us to say "No" to ungodliness and worldly passions, and to live self-controlled, upright and godly lives in this present age,
Titus 2:11-12 NIV

Daily Meditation:
Gracious God, thank You for the boundless grace and mercy. Empower me to live a life marked by godliness, embracing the transformative influence of Your grace and walking in righteousness, guided by the teachings of Your Word

Additional Readings:
1 Timothy 2:3-5 | Ezekiel 18:23

Bible in a year:
Joshua Chapters: 9-11

March 14th.

BUT EACH PERSON IS TEMPTED WHEN
THEY ARE DRAGGED AWAY BY THEIR
OWN EVIL DESIRE AND ENTICED.
THEN, AFTER DESIRE HAS CONCEIVED,
IT GIVES BIRTH TO SIN; AND SIN,
WHEN IT IS FULL-GROWN, GIVES
BIRTH TO DEATH.
JAMES 1:14-15 NIV

Daily Meditation:
Lord, help me to resist the allure of temptation, recognizing
that it gives birth to sin and ultimately leads me away from
Your perfect plan, for my life. May Your grace be my anchor,
helping me overcome the pull of earthly desires.

Additional Readings:
Genesis 2:17 | Proverbs 11:19

Bible in a year:
Joshua Chapters: 12-15

March 15th.

WHEN TEMPTED, NO ONE SHOULD
SAY, "GOD IS TEMPTING ME." FOR GOD
CANNOT BE TEMPTED BY EVIL, NOR
DOES HE TEMPT ANYONE;

JAMES 1:13 NIV

Daily Meditation:

Lord, when I face trials and temptations, I know that You are
not the source of these challenges. You are a God of
goodness and not of evil. Strengthen me to resist
temptation and to seek Your guidance in all I do.

Additional Readings:

1 Corinthians 10:13 | Mark 14:38

Bible in a year:

Joshua Chapters: 16-18

March 16th.

My dear brothers and sisters, take note of this: Everyone should be quick to listen, slow to speak and slow to become angry, because human anger does not produce the righteousness that God desires.

James 1:19-20 NIV

Daily Meditation:
Dear God, grant me the patience to listen well, humility to receive Your Word, and self-control to hold my tongue. Help me reflect Your love in my actions and restrain any anger that may hinder the righteousness You desire in my life.

Additional Readings:
Proverbs 10:19 | Proverbs 17:27

Bible in a year:
Joshua Chapters: 19-21

March 17th.

BUT WHOEVER LOOKS INTENTLY INTO
THE PERFECT LAW THAT GIVES
FREEDOM, AND CONTINUES IN IT NOT
FORGETTING WHAT THEY HAVE
HEARD, BUT DOING IT, THEY WILL BE
BLESSED IN WHAT THEY DO.

JAMES 1:25 NIV

Daily Meditation:
Heavenly Father, thank You for the healing power of Your word. May I persevere to consistently walk in Your truth, finding joy in the freedom and blessings that come from applying Your teachings to every aspect of my life.

Additional Readings:
Romans 2:13 | James 1:23-24

Bible in a year:
Joshua Chapters: 22-24

March 18th.

THOSE WHO CONSIDER THEMSELVES RELIGIOUS AND YET DO NOT KEEP A TIGHT REIN ON THEIR TONGUES DECEIVE THEMSELVES, AND THEIR RELIGION IS WORTHLESS.

JAMES 1:26 NIV

Daily Meditation:
Lord, may the words I speak be a reflection of a heart devoted to You. Help me guard my tongue, and may my conversations overflow with grace, kindness, and the love that stems from a genuine faith in You.

Additional Readings:
Psalm 34:13 | Psalm 141:3

Bible in a year:
Judges Chapters: 1-2

March 19th.

Blessed is the man who does not walk in the counsel of the wicked, or set foot on the path of sinners, or sit in the seat of mockers. But his delight is in the Law of the LORD, and on His law he meditates day and night. He is like a tree planted by streams of water, yielding its fruit in season, whose leaf does not wither, and who prospers in all he does.

Psalm 1:1-2 BSB

Daily Meditation:

Lord, help me to delight in Your word and meditate on it continually. May it be the foundation of my thoughts, actions, and decisions. Grant me discernment to avoid the paths of unrighteousness. Strengthen my faith and lead me.

Additional Readings:

Joshua 1:8 | Psalm 119:1-8

Bible in a year:

Judges Chapters: 3-5

March 20th.

FOR THE SPIRIT GOD GAVE US DOES NOT MAKE US TIMID, BUT GIVES US POWER, LOVE AND SELF-DISCIPLINE.
2 TIMOTHY 1:7 NIV

Daily Meditation:
Holy Spirit, I ask for You to strengthen me, body, mind and spirit. Let fear find no place in my heart. Help me to live boldly, loving others with Your grace and wisdom.

Additional Readings:
Isaiah 11:2 | Luke 10:19

Bible in a year:
Judges Chapters: 6-7

March 21st.

He has saved us and called us to a holy life, not because of anything we have done but because of his own purpose and grace. This grace was given us in Christ Jesus before the beginning of time,
2 Timothy 1:9 NIV

Daily Meditation:
Gracious Father, thank You for calling me by Your grace. Guide me in living out this divine calling, rooted in Your mercy, and may my life be a testimony to Your unchanging love and sovereign plan.

Additional Readings:
Romans 8:29-30 | Ephesians 1:4

Bible in a year:
Judges Chapters: 8-9

March 22nd.

FINALLY, BROTHERS AND SISTERS, WHATEVER IS TRUE, WHATEVER IS NOBLE, WHATEVER IS RIGHT, WHATEVER IS PURE, WHATEVER IS LOVELY, WHATEVER IS ADMIRABLE IF ANYTHING IS EXCELLENT OR PRAISEWORTHY THINK ABOUT SUCH THINGS.

PHILLIPPIANS 4:8 NIV

Daily Meditation:
Jesus, let the meditation of my heart and my thoughts be aligned in truth and goodness. Let my anxieties of this life fade away when I focus on You and Your word.

Additional Readings:
1 Timothy 4:12 | Roman's 14:18-19

Bible in a year:
Judges Chapters: 10-12

March 23rd.

WHATEVER YOU HAVE LEARNED OR
RECEIVED OR HEARD FROM ME, OR
SEEN IN ME, PUT IT INTO PRACTICE.
AND THE GOD OF PEACE WILL BE
WITH YOU.
PHILIPPIANS 4:9 NIV

Daily Meditation:
Lord Jesus, I don't just want to hear Your words, I want them
them to seep down into my inner most being and become
what I live, breathe and do so that I may rest in Your peace.

Additional Readings:
Matthew 7:15-23

Bible in a year:
Judges Chapters: 13-15

March 24th.

Cast all Your anxiety on him
because he cares for you. Be alert
and of sober mind. Your enemy
the devil prowls around like a
roaring lion looking for
someone to devour.
1 Peter 5:7-8 niv

Daily Meditation:
Jesus, I know that just being Your child makes me a walking
target for temptation and struggling with my flesh. Lord I
claim Your power and authority over my life as provision
and protection in times of trouble.

Additional Readings:
Isaiah 41:9-11 | Ephesians 6:10-17

Bible in a year:
Judges Chapters: 16-18

March 25th.

Do you not know that in a race all the runners run, but only one gets the prize? Run in such a way as to get the prize. Everyone who competes in the games goes into strict training. They do it to get a crown that will not last, but we do it to get a crown that will last forever.
1 Corinthians 9:24-25 NIV

Daily Meditation:
Jesus, when I get to the end of this life, I want my goal to have been to walk closely and intimately with You to know that even though I am not perfect, I am Your dearly loved child. I long to hear hear you say "Well done."

Additional Readings:
Philippians 3:12-21

Bible in a year:
Judges Chapters: 19-21

March 26th.

THEREFORE I DO NOT RUN LIKE SOMEONE RUNNING AIMLESSLY; I DO NOT FIGHT LIKE A BOXER BEATING THE AIR. NO, I STRIKE A BLOW TO MY BODY AND MAKE IT MY SLAVE SO THAT AFTER I HAVE PREACHED TO OTHERS, I MYSELF WILL NOT BE DISQUALIFIED FOR THE PRIZE.

1 CORINTHIANS 9:26-27 NIV

Daily Meditation:
Father help me to deny the temptation of my body, may my words and actions be informed and aligned by Your will and purpose for my life. Thank You for Your forgiveness and healing over my struggles.

Additional Readings:
2 Timothy 4:7-9 | James 1:12

Bible in a year:
Book of Ruth

March 27th.

Do you not know that your bodies
are temples of the Holy Spirit,
who is in you, whom you have
received from God? You are not
your own; you were bought at a
price. Therefore honor God
with your bodies.
1 Corinthians 6:19-20 niv

Daily Meditation:
Jesus, in acknowledgment of Your sacrifice for my sin and
redeeming my soul; I offer myself as a living sacrifice. I ask
that Your anointing would be on me and that Your wisdom
would flow from me; that you would use me as you see fit.

Additional Readings:
Isaiah 44:22 | Romans 13:13

Bible in a year:
1 Samuel Chapters: 1-3

March 28th.

His divine power has given us everything we need for a godly life through our knowledge of him who called us by his own glory and goodness.

2 Peter 1:3 NIV

Daily Meditation:
Lord, the fact that You called me alone leaves me in awe and wonder of Your grace and goodness. Thank You for leading me and for providing an abundant life in You.

Additional Readings:
Psalm 84:11 | 1 Thessalonians 2:12

Bible in a year:
1 Samuel Chapters: 4-8

March 29th.

THROUGH THESE HE HAS GIVEN US HIS
VERY GREAT AND PRECIOUS PROMISES,
SO THAT THROUGH THEM YOU MAY
PARTICIPATE IN THE DIVINE NATURE,
HAVING ESCAPED THE CORRUPTION IN
THE WORLD CAUSED BY EVIL DESIRES.
2 PETER 1:4 NIV

Daily Meditation:
Heavenly Father, I thank You that I have the privilege to
partake in Your divine nature and escape the corruption in
the world caused by evil desires. Help me to strengthen my
faith and guide me to live a life worthy of Your calling.

Additional Readings:
Ephesians 4:13 | Galatians 6:8

Bible in a year:
1 Samuel Chapters: 9-12

March 30th.

FOR THIS VERY REASON, MAKE EVERY EFFORT TO ADD TO YOUR FAITH GOODNESS; AND TO GOODNESS, KNOWLEDGE; AND TO KNOWLEDGE, SELF-CONTROL; AND TO SELF-CONTROL, PERSEVERANCE; AND TO PERSEVERANCE, GODLINESS; AND TO GODLINESS, MUTUAL AFFECTION; AND TO MUTUAL AFFECTION, LOVE.
2 PETER 1:5-7 NIV

Daily Meditation:
Jesus, as I grow and mature in the love You have given me, I pray for gentle pruning to make me more like You. Let me not stray far from You; so that my life will be full of Your goodness, guidance and blessings.

Additional Readings:
John 15:1-4 | 1 Corinthians 15:58

Bible in a year:
1 Samuel Chapters: 13-14

March 31st.

THE MORE YOU GROW LIKE THIS, THE
MORE PRODUCTIVE AND USEFUL YOU
WILL BE IN OUR KNOWLEDGE OF OUR
LORD JESUS CHRIST. BUT THOSE WHO
FAIL TO DEVELOP IN THIS WAY ARE
SHORTSIGHTED OR BLIND, FORGETTING
THAT THEY HAVE BEEN CLEANSED FROM
THEIR OLD SINS.
2 PETER 1:8-9 NLT

Daily Meditation:
Holy Spirit, help me to grow and be attuned to Your will; so
that I may do work for the kingdom. May my life be
abundant with fruit to bless others and leave
a ripple for the future.

Additional Readings:
2 Peter 1:10 | Matthew 25:26

Bible in a year:
1 Samuel Chapters: 15-17

www.ingramcontent.com/pod-product-compliance
Lightning Source LLC
Chambersburg PA
CBHW062008040426
42447CB00010B/1962